Johnny Ruffo

The biography of Home and Away' actor and singer, cause of death and legacy

James C. Rosales

Table of contents

Chapter 1:Early Life and Career

Chapter 2. The X Factor and Music Career

Chapter 3. Acting Career

Chapter 4. Personal Life

Chapter 5. Legacy and Tributes

Chapter 1:Early Life and Career

Johnny Ruffo, born on March 8, 1988, in Balcatta, a suburb of Perth, Western Australia, began his journey in a modest setting. Raised by his parents Jill and Pascoe Ruffo, their separation when he was three led him to spend most of his youth in a small Homeswest unit with his mother. Despite the challenges, Ruffo attended Balcatta Senior High School, laying the groundwork for his future.

The spark of Ruffo's musical journey ignited at the age of 12 when he discovered his passion for music, inspired by the legendary Michael Jackson. His early interest in the art led him to self-learn the guitar and piano, and remarkably, he crafted his first song at the tender age of 14. Beyond Jackson, Ruffo drew inspiration from contemporary artists such as Justin Timberlake, Usher, and Chris Brown, shaping his evolving musical style.

Before making waves in the music industry, Ruffo ventured into the world of concreting, a profession he entered thanks to his father's involvement in the trade. Simultaneously, he showcased his musical talents by performing around Perth with the electropop band Supanova. This dual life showcased Ruffo's dedication and diverse skill set.

In 2011, Ruffo decided to take a leap of faith by auditioning for the third season of The X Factor Australia. His rendition of Jay Sean's "Do You Remember" caught the attention of the judges, earning him a spot in the competition. Mentored by Guy Sebastian, Ruffo progressed to the live shows, where his performances resonated with audiences. Although he finished in third place, with Reece Mastin securing the top spot, Ruffo's journey on The X Factor marked a turning point in his career.

Following the competition, Ruffo's talent was quickly recognized, leading to a recording contract with Sony Music Australia. This milestone marked the beginning of his official foray into the music industry. The exposure gained from The X Factor, coupled with his innate musical abilities, positioned Ruffo as a rising star with the potential for a promising career.

Chapter 2. The X Factor and Music Career

Johnny Ruffo's journey through The X Factor and his subsequent music career is a captivating narrative of talent, resilience, and the pursuit of artistic success. Auditioning for the third season of The X Factor Australia in 2011, Ruffo's rendition of Jay Sean's "Do You Remember" not only impressed the judges but also set the stage for a remarkable journey in the music industry. The positive feedback he received from all four judges, praising his vocals, charisma, and stage presence, propelled him forward to the bootcamp stage, where he further showcased his talent with performances of Chris Brown's "With You" and Lady Gaga's "The Edge of Glory."

Selected by Guy Sebastian as one of his top three boys for the live shows, Ruffo's performances throughout the competition were marked by versatility and energy. Notable moments include his renditions of Maroon 5's "Moves Like Jagger," Meat Loaf's "I'd Do Anything for Love (But I Won't Do That)," Justin Timberlake's "What Goes Around... Comes Around," and Stevie Wonder's "Sir Duke." His ability to captivate both judges and viewers allowed him to navigate through challenges, surviving two sing-offs against Declan Sykes and Three Wishez with performances of Bruno Mars' "Just the Way You Are" and Michael Jackson's "Billie Jean," respectively.

Reaching the grand final, Ruffo showcased his journey by reprising his audition song "Do You Remember," performing his winner's single "You Don't Wanna Know," and engaging in memorable duets with Salt-N-Pepa on "Shoop" and "Push It." Despite finishing in third place behind Andrew Wishart and Reece Mastin, Ruffo's time on The X Factor became a launching pad for his music career.

Following his exit from The X Factor, Ruffo signed a recording contract with Sony Music Australia, marking a pivotal moment in his professional trajectory. His enthusiasm for this new chapter was evident as he expressed being "thrilled" to join the label and teased "a lot of exciting things" planned for his music career. Grateful for the support of his fans, he looked forward to sharing his music with them.

Ruffo's debut single, "On Top," released on June 15, 2012, quickly made its mark, peaking at number 14 on the ARIA Singles Chart and earning platinum certification from the Australian Recording Industry Association (ARIA). Co-written with Anthony Egizii and David Musumeci, the song reflected Ruffo's personality and style as an artist, conveying a message about having fun with friends and living life to the fullest.

Continuing his musical journey, Ruffo released his second single, "Take It Home," on November 2, 2012. This more mature track, co-written with Ilan Kidron and Louis

Schoorl, peaked at number 29 on the ARIA Singles Chart and received gold certification from ARIA. The song delved into themes of finding that special someone and taking them home.

"Untouchable," Ruffo's third single released on March 15, 2013, explored the realm of love. Co-written with Anthony Egizii, David Musumeci, and Cassie Davis, the song peaked at number 63 on the ARIA Singles Chart. Ruffo described it as a love song, emphasizing the emotions associated with being with someone who makes you feel untouchable.

The release of "She Got That O" on September 13, 2013, marked Ruffo's fourth single. Co-written with Anthony Egizii,

David Musumeci, and Israel Cruz, the track, characterized as a fun, upbeat party anthem, peaked at number 87 on the ARIA Singles Chart. It celebrated the uniqueness of a girl who stands out from the crowd.

Ruffo's fifth single, "So Far Gone," released on May 9, 2014, explored personal emotions within the context of a relationship gone sour. Despite not charting on the ARIA Singles Chart, the song showcased Ruffo's ability to delve into more introspective and emotional themes. This period also saw the release of his debut extended play (EP) titled "Untouchable" on August 15, 2014. The EP peaked at number 27 on the ARIA Albums Chart and received gold certification from ARIA. Featuring six songs, including his previous singles and two new tracks,

"Timeless" and "Don't Wanna Let You Down," the EP encapsulated Ruffo's diverse musical influences spanning pop, R&B, dance, and hip hop.

Throughout his music career, Ruffo collaborated with various artists, demonstrating his versatility and willingness to explore different genres. His features on songs like "Turn It Up" by Israel Cruz, "Live It Up" by Samantha Jade, and "Dancefloor" by DJ Havana Brown added layers to his musical repertoire. These collaborations showcased his ability to contribute to diverse sounds, from club bangers to feel-good anthems.

Ruffo's presence extended beyond recorded tracks, as he embraced live performances and touring. Supporting One Direction on their Up All Night Tour in April 2012, opening for New Kids on the Block and Backstreet Boys on their NKOTBSB Tour in May 2012, and warming up the crowd for Mariah Carey on her The Elusive Chanteuse Show in November 2014 highlighted Ruffo's ability to connect with diverse audiences. Headlining his own national tour in September and October 2012, he engaged with fans, promising surprises and showcasing the dynamic range of his music.

In addition to major tours, Ruffo graced events like the Sydney Gay and Lesbian Mardi Gras in March 2013, the Nickelodeon Slimefest in September 2013, and the Carols by Candlelight in December 2013. Each performance demonstrated his love for entertaining people with his music and his ability to adapt his style to different occasions.

Johnny Ruffo's journey from The X Factor to a flourishing music career is a testament to his artistic evolution, determination, and ability to resonate with audiences. His early life, marked by modest beginnings and a passion for music, laid the foundation for a career that spanned chart-topping singles, gold and platinum certifications, collaborations with renowned artists, and unforgettable live performances. As Ruffo's music continues to echo in the hearts of his fans, his story stands as an inspiring chapter in the annals of the Australian music scene.

Chapter 3. Acting Career

Johnny Ruffo's venture into the realm of acting added a new dimension to his already diverse career, showcasing his versatility and ability to excel in different artistic domains.

In 2013, Ruffo made a significant leap into the world of television by landing a role on the popular Australian soap opera, Home and Away. Cast as Chris Harrington, the brother of Spencer Harrington (played by Andrew J Morley), Ruffo's portrayal of the character was notable for its cheeky charm and flirtatious demeanor. The role, reportedly inspired by Ruffo's own personality, resonated with viewers as he navigated the complexities of relationships and stirred the pot in Summer Bay. His on-screen chemistry extended beyond romantic entanglements, as his character developed a close friendship with Irene Roberts, portrayed by Lynne McGranger, who became his surrogate mother on the show.

Ruffo's tenure on Home and Away spanned three years, culminating in his departure in 2016. Expressing a desire to explore other opportunities, he bid farewell to the iconic series that had become a significant chapter in his acting journey.

Before his stint on Home and Away, Ruffo dipped his toes into the world of film with a cameo appearance in the 2012 movie, The Sapphires. In this film, he played the role of a Vietnam soldier, showcasing his ability to seamlessly transition between different mediums of entertainment.

Further expanding his presence on the small screen, Ruffo hosted the X Factor spin-off show, X-Stream, in 2011. This experience not only highlighted his charisma and comfort in front of the camera but also hinted at his growing potential as a multifaceted entertainer.

In 2017, Ruffo took on the role of Tommy in the Channel Nine mini-series House of Bond, a portrayal that added another layer to his acting repertoire. The mini-series depicted the life of Alan Bond, with Ruffo's character offering a unique perspective on the narrative.

Not limiting himself to one genre or format, Ruffo continued to embrace acting opportunities. In 2020, he appeared in two episodes of the long-running Australian soap opera, Neighbours, as Owen Campbell. His character, a love interest for Bea Nilsson (played by Bonnie Anderson), showcased Ruffo's ability to bring depth and authenticity to his roles.

Balancing his music and acting careers, Ruffo demonstrated a remarkable ability to seamlessly navigate between these two creative realms. His journey in the music industry began with a strong presence on The X Factor Australia in 2011, where he finished third and subsequently signed a recording contract with Sony Music

Australia. The success of his debut single, "On Top," which peaked at number 14 on the ARIA Singles Chart and received platinum certification, solidified his position in the music scene.

Ruffo continued to release singles, including "Take It Home" and "Untouchable," and actively participated in major musical events, supporting internationally acclaimed acts like One Direction and the Backstreet Boys during their Australian tours. This dual commitment to music and acting showcased his passion for both art forms.

Despite facing health issues that delayed the release of his debut album, Ruffo remained resolute in pursuing his artistic endeavors. His dedication to both music and acting highlighted a commitment to delivering quality performances across various platforms.

Johnny Ruffo's ability to seamlessly transition between music and acting, coupled with his magnetic on-screen presence, solidifies his status as a multifaceted artist. From the stage of The X Factor to the shores of Summer Bay and beyond, Ruffo's journey stands as a testament to the boundless possibilities that arise when talent, passion, and versatility converge in the world of entertainment.

Chapter 4. Personal Life

Johnny Ruffo's personal life is marked by a tapestry of relationships, health struggles, and a resilient spirit that left an indelible mark on those who followed his journey. Born in Balcatta, a suburb of Perth, Western Australia, Ruffo's early life was shaped by the separation of his parents, Jill and Pascoe Ruffo, when he was just three years old. This experience laid the foundation for the strong bond he shares with his brother Michael, who resides in Ireland and serves as his closest confidante.

In matters of the heart, Ruffo has navigated through high-profile relationships, including those with Home and Away actresses Samara Weaving and Jessica Grace Smith.

However, as of the latest updates, he is currently single and not publicly dating anyone. Amid the twists and turns of romance, one constant in Ruffo's life has been his girlfriend, Tahnee Sims, a steadfast presence by his side throughout his challenging cancer journey.

The onset of Ruffo's health struggles began in 2017 when he received a devastating diagnosis of brain cancer. Undertaking emergency surgery to remove a tumor from his brain, he displayed incredible resilience, making a full recovery and resuming his pursuits in acting and music. Despite this triumph, the specter of cancer returned in November 2020, with Ruffo sharing the heartbreaking news that his condition was now terminal.

Undeterred, Ruffo embarked on a courageous battle against the disease, undergoing chemotherapy injections every three weeks and maintaining a regimen of regular check-ups and MRIs. His openness and honesty about his cancer journey became a source of inspiration for many, as he shared the highs and lows with fans through social media and various media appearances.

In December 2020, Ruffo shared the hopeful news that he had completed his chemotherapy treatment for the year, expressing anticipation for quality time with his family. However, the rollercoaster of his health continued, with a March 2021 update from the hospital indicating his return to the familiar routine of chemotherapy.

Tragically, on November 10, 2023, Johnny Ruffo passed away at the age of 35, succumbing to the relentless battle against cancer. His family confirmed the news, marking the end of a journey that inspired countless individuals facing their own health challenges.

Beyond the personal struggles, Ruffo used his platform to raise awareness about cancer, participating in documentaries like 7News Spotlight and The Morning Show. His advocacy extended to the written word with the release of his book, "No Finish Line," providing an intimate look into his life story, fame, and the formidable hurdles posed by cancer.

While facing the harsh realities of a terminal illness, Ruffo remained steadfast in his pursuit of passion. He continued to contribute to the worlds of music and acting, releasing new songs and making appearances in TV shows like House of Bond and Neighbours. His commitment to creativity and expression in the face of adversity showcased the depth of his character.

Throughout his journey, Ruffo consistently expressed gratitude for the unwavering support and love he received from family, friends, and fans. His public statements reflected a resilient spirit, with a stated goal of living a happy life and helping as many people as possible along the way.

In the end, Johnny Ruffo's life was a testament to the intertwining threads of love, loss, courage, and creativity. His legacy extends beyond the stages he graced and the music he shared, leaving an enduring impact on those who admired his talent and drew strength from his unyielding spirit in the face of life's most formidable challenges.

Chapter 5. Legacy and Tributes

Johnny Ruffo was a talented singer, actor, and dancer who left a lasting impact on the Australian music and entertainment industry. He rose to fame as a finalist on The X Factor Australia in 2011, where he impressed the judges and audiences with his charisma and vocal skills. He then pursued a successful career as a recording artist, releasing several singles and touring with One Direction and New Kids on the Block. He also ventured into acting, landing a role as Chris Harrington on the popular soap opera Home and Away from 2013 to 2016. He won the hearts of many fans with his charming and funny personality, as well as his advocacy for various causes such as Starlight Children's Foundation and Cancer Council.

Johnny Ruffo's legacy and tributes are as follows:

- Impact on Australian music and entertainment: Johnny Ruffo was a versatile and talented performer who contributed to the Australian music and entertainment scene in various ways. He was known for his catchy pop songs, such as On Top, Take It Home, and Untouchable, which showcased his vocal range and style. He also collaborated with other artists, such as rapper Illy on the track Tightrope, and DJ Havana Brown on the dance anthem Whatever We Want. He was nominated for several awards, such as the ARIA Music

Awards, the Nickelodeon Kids' Choice Awards, and the World Music Awards. He also demonstrated his acting skills on Home and Away, where he played a lovable and loyal character who faced many challenges and dramas. He won the Logie Award for Most Popular New Male Talent in 2014, and was nominated for the Silver Logie for Most Popular Actor in 2015 and 2016. He also participated in other shows, such as Dancing with the Stars, where he finished third in 2012, and Celebrity Apprentice Australia, where he raised money for the Starlight Children's Foundation in 2023.

- Tributes from fans and colleagues: Johnny Ruffo's fans and colleagues expressed their love and support for him throughout his battle with brain cancer, which he first revealed in 2017. He received many messages of encouragement and admiration from his followers on social media, who praised him for his courage and positivity. He also received tributes from his fellow celebrities and friends, who shared their memories and appreciation of him. Some of the notable tributes include:

- Carrie Bickmore, who interviewed him on The Project in 2023, wrote on Instagram: "Oh Johnny....Sending so much love. Kick it's arse "

- Lincoln Lewis, who co-starred with him on Home and Away, wrote on Instagram: "F### man we're all here with you and cheering you on!!! Sending all our love, support and good energy brother!! You got this ¹l"

- Georgie Parker, who also co-starred with him on Home and Away, wrote on Instagram: "Yes you will. I love you so much, Johnny.
"

- Dan Ewing, who also co-starred with him on Home and Away, wrote on Instagram: "Let's get after it Ruffo!! "

- Penny McNamee, who also co-starred with him on Home and Away, wrote on Instagram: "Will be praying for you Johnny. You have an enormous amount of love and support."

- Tahnee Sims, his girlfriend of six years, wrote on Instagram: "Thank you for all the amazing memories babe "

Printed in Great Britain
by Amazon

32693582R00020